A Visit to
FRANCE

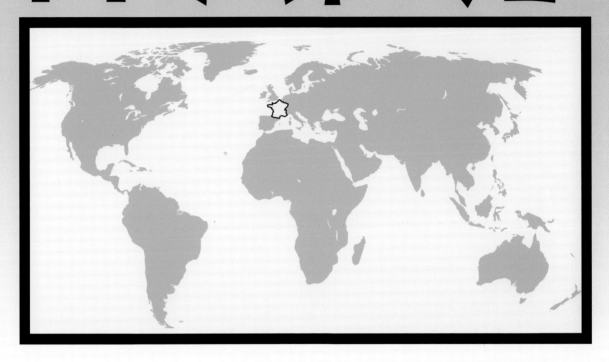

Rob Alcraft

Heinemann Library
Des Plaines, Illinois

© 1999 Reed Educational & Professional Publishing
Published by Heinemann Library,
an imprint of Reed Educational & Professional Publishing,
1350 East Touhy Avenue, Suite 240 West
Des Plaines, IL 60018

Customer Service 1-888-454-2279

Designed by AMR
Illustrations by Art Construction
Printed in Hong Kong/China

03 02 01 00 99
10 9 8 7 6 5 4 3 2 1

Library of Congress Cataloging-in-Publication Data

Alcraft, Rob, 1966-
   A visit to France / Rob Alcraft.
     p. cm. -- (Visit to)
   Includes bibliographical references and index.
   ISBN 1-51572-851-6 (lib. bdg.)
   1. France--Pictorial works--Juvenile literature. I. Title.
   II. Title: France. III. Series.
   DC20.A55 1999
   944—dc21   99-19129
                                                  CIP

Acknowledgments
The Publishers would like to thank the following for permission to reproduce photographs:
Bridgeman Art Library, p. 28; Image Bank, p.18; J. Allan Cash, pp. 17, 25; Rex Features, Sipa Press, p. 29; Robert Harding Picture Library, p. 9; Robert Francis, p. 5; Adam Woolfitt, p. 6; Nik Wheeler, p. 15; K. Gillham, p. 21; Tomlinson, p. 26; Telegraph Color Library , C. B. Knight, p. 16; Richard Cooke, p. 19; Kathy Collins, p. 27; Trevor Clifford, pp. 13, 17; Trip/D. Hastilow, p. 7; A. Tovy, p. 8; J. Braund, p. 10; P. Rauter, p. 11; A. M. Bazalik p. 12; Ask Images p. 22; S. Grant, p. 20; R. Cracknell, p. 23; B. Gadsby, p. 24.

Cover photo: Eye Ubiquitous/H. Hedworth

Any words appearing in bold, **like this**, are explained in the Glossary.

Contents

France

France is a country in Europe.

The French people eat, sleep, go to
school, and play like you. Life in
France is also **unique**.

Land

There are green fields and **meadows** in northern France. The weather is cool, and it often rains. Farmers grow **wheat** and keep cows.

There are high mountains in southern France. In the mountains, it is cool and wet. By the Mediterranean Sea, it is sunny and dry.

Landmarks

This is the Eiffel Tower. It is in the middle of Paris. Paris is France's **capital** city. It is the biggest city in France.

This is a bridge called the Pont du Gard.
It was built to carry water to an ancient
city. The bridge is 2,000 years old.

Homes

Most people in the cities live in apartment buildings. Windows have wooden **shutters** to keep the rooms cool in summer.

Many smaller towns and villages in France are very old. There are shady **squares** and narrow streets. There are old houses built from stone.

Food

Each **region** of France makes its own kind of cheese and sausage. A good snack is cheese and a long stick of French bread. The bread is very fresh and the crust is crisp.

French families sit together to eat. This family is enjoying a simple breakfast of bread and jam.

Clothes

Many young French people wear jeans
and sneakers. They wear colorful T-shirts,
sweaters, and coats. Some older people
wear a French hat called a *beret* (ber-AY).

For festivals and parties, people dress up in old French costumes. Women wear white blouses, **bonnets**, and long black skirts with colorful patterns.

Work

France is famous for its **fashion**.
Some people have jobs in the fashion
business. They make and sell clothes.

In the country, many farmers grow grapes or olive trees. The olives are eaten or pressed into cooking oil.

Transportation

France has fast **highways**. People pay **tolls** to use them. The busiest highway goes in a big loop around Paris.

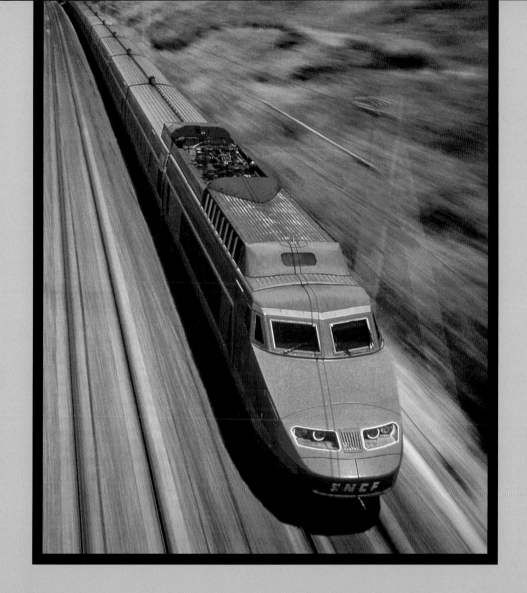

French trains are comfortable and very fast. They can go three times faster than a car. Most cities have airports. France also has **canals** and rivers busy with **barges**.

Language

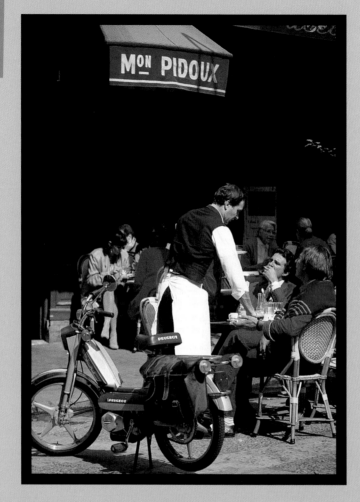

The people speak French. French
sounds different from English, but it
uses the same alphabet. It is written in
the same way, too, from left to right.

Different **regions** of France have their own **dialects**. French is also spoken in many places around the world.

School

Children go to school six days a week in most of France. There is no school on Wednesday afternoons. French children study math, geography, and English.

Some French schools have special
vacations. The whole class will have
lessons by the beach for a week. In the
winter, the class might learn how to ski.

Free Time

Young people play sports, such as soccer, in the parks. Sometimes they watch TV or visit friends. In the summer, they might swim at the beach or in the river.

On warm, summer evenings, many French people like to sit in the **cafés** and watch people go by. Some people play a bowling game, called **pétanque,** in the market **squares**.

Celebrations

One of the biggest celebrations in France is called Mardi Gras. Everyone has a big party. There are fireworks and **parades** along the city streets.

Many French towns and villages have their own special celebration. They might celebrate a Saint's Day or the **harvest**. Some towns hold a celebration in honor of their cheese.

The Arts

There have been many famous French painters. This is a painting by Renoir. He wanted his paintings to show how beautiful and colorful the world is.

Making movies is important in France.
In May, there is a special film festival in a
town called *Cannes*. People come from all
over the world to see the new movies.

Fact File

Name	The French Republic is the country's full name.
Capital	France's **capital** city is called Paris.
Language	The people speak French.
Population	There are about 58 million people living in France.
Money	French money is called the franc.
Religion	Most French people are Christians, but there are many other religions, too.
Products	France makes cars, cloth, aircraft, machines, and **electrical goods**. **Tourism** is also very important.

Words You Can Learn

bonjour (bon-jewer)	hello
au revoir (oh-rev-wa)	goodbye
oui (we)	yes
non (noh)	no
merci (ma-r-see)	thank you
s'il vous plaît (see voo play)	please
un (urn)	one
deux (de)	two
trois (twa)	three

Glossary

barge	Boat with a flat bottom. It can float in shallow water.
bonnet	Kind of hat worn by women
café	Shop that sells coffee and snacks
canal	River dug by people
capital	City where the government is based
dialect	Special way people in one area say and use the words of their language
electrical goods	Things such as TVs and VCRs that use electricity
fashion	The way clothes are made and shaped, and how they look
harvest	Time when fruit, vegetables, and corn are ready for the farmer to pick
highway	Big, fast road. Often there are three lanes of cars going each way.
meadow	Grassy land
parade	Special carnival in the street
pétanque	Game like bowling
region	Part of a country
shutter	Wooden flap along side of a window. Shutters can be closed to keep out the light, heat, or wind.
square	Open space in a city with streets on all four sides
toll	Money that is paid to drive on a special road
tourism	Everything to do with visiting a place while on vacation
unique	Different in a special way
wheat	Grasslike plant used to make flour

Index

More Books to Read

Arnold, Helen. *France.* Chatham, N.J.: Raintree Steck-Vaughn, 1995.

Gamgee, John. (Ed.) *Journey Through France.* Mahwah, N.J.: Troll Communications, 1997. An older reader can help you with this book.

Streissguth, Thomas. *France.* Minneapolis, Minn: Lerner Publishing Group, 1997. An older reader can help you with this book.